LEGALISM

THE ETHICAL SYSTEM THAT BECOMES A FALSE GOD

L. J. ANDERSON

LAMAD PRESS

CONTENTS

**To every believer who's been called a legalist
or Pharisee for simply obeying Scripture:**
May you never confuse obedience with performance,
nor let the fear of man silence your pursuit of holiness.

ABSTRACT

This book critically examines legalism as both an ethical and salvific system, exposing its theological flaws while acknowledging its practical appeal. Though often used loosely in Christian discourse, legalism is a coherent moral framework, one that offers structure, clarity, and a high view of obedience. Yet Scripture consistently portrays it as a distortion of true righteousness. By analyzing legalism's strengths and weaknesses, this work demonstrates why it must be rejected: not because it values obedience, but because it replaces relational faithfulness with rule-based righteousness.

Drawing from biblical texts, historical theology, and contemporary ethical theory, *Legalism* argues that God demands not mere outward conformity, but inward transformation motivated by love. True obedience flows from relationship, not rigid systems. This work challenges the modern church to rethink the simplistic binary of legalism versus antinomianism and calls for a biblical ethic grounded in love, loyalty, and divine authority.

While this book stands on its own as a critique of legalism, it also serves as an intellectual and theological foundation for the forthcoming volume *Salvation by Faith Alone?*, where the relationship between faith, works, and salvation will be examined in greater detail.

PREFACE

The book you are reading is the result of scholarly research presented in a format accessible to the general public. Normally, a work like this would not be published in this form. It would almost certainly appear as a journal article—technically accessible, but realistically out of reach for most Christians. This is simply because very few Christians who haven't attended Bible college read academic journal articles in their pursuit of God. However, many do read books.

Even pastors often find it difficult to engage with journal articles regularly, though they may have a large collection of books. Presenting research in book form, similar in depth and length to a journal article, means it can potentially reach a much broader audience. That is why virtually all of my journal-length writings are, or will be, published as short books. My goal is to provide solid academic research without requiring readers to locate or gain access to academic journals.

Additionally, I hope more authors and scholars will join me in this endeavor. Independent publishing offers many benefits and only a few significant drawbacks, namely, the lack of peer review and brand recognition. Authors who are not yet widely known often depend on the credibility of the publisher's name. Peer review, for its part, plays an important role in academic publishing, acting as a gatekeeper to prevent poor scholarship from reaching publication. Where possible, I welcome peer-reviewed engagement with these ideas in journal articles, responses, and academic dialogue.

However, peer review does not guarantee high-quality work, just as the absence of peer review does not necessarily imply poor quality. In many ways, true peer review begins after publication, when the broader academic community has the opportunity to evaluate and respond to the work. In this model, peer engagement happens post-publication, as scholars interact with the material in print, online forums, public reviews, and future publications.

While still largely untested, this publishing model shows promise as an alternative method of making academic research accessible. The majority of scholars continue to view independent publishing as significantly inferior to peer-reviewed articles or works released by traditional academic presses.

The following note expands on the mission behind Lamad Press and my broader goals as an independent scholar-publisher.

Theological Publishing with Purpose

L. J. Anderson is pioneering a new approach to theological scholarship, one that is academically rigorous, biblically faithful, and institutionally independent.

Through Lamad Press, he is constructing a publishing model that restores Scripture as the primary authority in theological method while engaging seriously with the philosophical and historical challenges of Christian doctrine. His work seeks not merely to critique existing systems but to build constructive theological models that speak to the most enduring tensions in Christian thought.

At the heart of this mission is Anderson's development of Structural Theism, a theological framework that accounts for the internal identity of God by emphasizing divine structure over classical simplicity. Structural Theism affirms the reality of Trinitarian distinction, upholds the relational depth of God revealed in Scripture, and seeks to avoid the conceptual pitfalls of both eternal generation and impersonal metaphysics. It is a model designed to preserve God's oneness and threeness without collapsing into modalism, metaphysical abstraction, or tritheism.

One key expression of this model is the Incarnational Monogenetic Model, which offers a biblically grounded alternative to the doctrine of eternal generation by locating the Son's identity not in timeless derivation, but in his incarnational role and mission as uniquely begotten of the Father.

Unlike traditional academic pathways bound by institutional gatekeeping and publishing delays, Anderson's independent model allows for timely, coherent, and accessible scholarship, published through Lamad Press and distributed by Lamad Christian Books. His aim is to demonstrate that it is possible to do theology that is both deeply scholarly and uncompromisingly biblical, outside the confines of conventional academic systems.

Rooted in Tradition

Independent theological publishing is not a modern innovation; rather, it is a return to Christian tradition. From the Church Fathers to the Reformers, many of the most influential theologians operated outside formal institutions, writing and distributing works grounded in theological conviction, fidelity to Scripture, and service to the church. Lamad Press stands in that same stream, reviving a historic model for a new generation of biblical theology.

CHAPTER ONE

A BRIEF INTRODUCTION AND HISTORY

L EGALISM IS A CONCEPT nearly every Christian has heard of, yet few take the time to define. It is a term that gets thrown around loosely. Sometimes it is to shame anyone who takes obedience seriously, other times to condemn traditions that seem overly rigid or outdated. But what exactly is legalism, and why is it so problematic? More importantly, why does Scripture seem to condemn it so strongly?

This book takes up that challenge. Legalism is not just a historical footnote in Pharisaic Judaism or a personality trait in overly zealous Christians. It is a full-fledged ethical system—a way of framing right and wrong, salvation and condemnation. And while it offers clarity, consistency, and even a surface-level respect for obedience, it ultimately replaces the authority of God with the authority of rules. It shifts the focus from the heart to external behavior, from divine relationship to human performance. And in doing so, it subtly redefines what it means to follow God with terrible consequences.

Historically, this system has crept into the church again and again, sometimes dressed in ritual, sometimes in doctrine, sometimes in cultural morality. Jesus' interactions with the Pharisees were not merely about misapplied laws; they were a direct confrontation with legalism as a counterfeit system of righteousness. When he said, "You tithe mint and dill and cumin, but neglect the weightier matters of the law" (Matthew 23:23), he wasn't calling them too obedient. He was calling them misaligned in their understanding of what obedience actually means.

Yet even with all its dangers, legalism persists for a reason: it offers benefits. It gives clear rules for what someone can and cannot do. It offers ethical simplicity, structure, and moral confidence. And in a world filled with ambiguity and compromise, that kind of clarity is attractive. We shouldn't pretend those benefits don't exist. But we also can't let them blind us to the deeper problems legalism creates, especially when it's allowed to distort our view of salvation.

This book begins by acknowledging the strengths of legalism so that we can dismantle it honestly. Then it exposes the deeper flaws: its inflexibility, its superficiality, its inability to address the human heart, and most of all, its contradiction of Scripture. Legalism ultimately presents itself as a path to righteousness; however, it cannot deliver. God hates true legalism not because he hates obedience, but because he demands something far deeper: love-motivated, Spirit-empowered, Christ-centered faithfulness. Legalism offers rules; God wants relationship. Legalism offers control; God calls for surrender.

What follows is not just a critique of an ethical system. It is a call to reframe how we think about obedience, ethics, and salvation itself. Legalism must be rejected, but not in favor of lawlessness. Rather, it must be replaced with a biblically grounded model of faith and obedience that flows from love for God and is grounded in the truth of his Word. As we will see, the problem isn't that legalism demands too much, but that it demands the wrong things and offers a false hope in return.

This book sets the stage for a larger and more urgent question: If legalism is not the answer, what is? If we are not saved by rule-keeping, are we saved by faith alone? And if so, what does that faith look like—and does obedience still matter? Those are the questions I take up in *Salvation by Faith Alone?* For now, we begin with the system many believe they've already rejected, but few truly understand.

CHAPTER TWO

POSITIVES OF LEGALISM

T HOUGH MANY MIGHT ARGUE that there is nothing
positive about legalism, the fact remains that this is
simply not true. The positives do not outweigh the nega-
tives by any means; however, it cannot be denied that legalism has benefits. It is imperative not to go misrepresent
legalism in this. Sinclair Ferguson writes, "'Isms' (such as
legalism and *antinomianism*) can be dangerous, not only
for those who espouse them but also for those who employ
the categories. They too easily become 'one size fits all'
pigeonholes."[1] This pitfall is something that ought to be
avoided.

It Is Simple to Follow with
Definite Answers to Ethical Problems

Legalism is all about having a rule for every possible situ-

---

1. Sinclair B. Ferguson, *The Whole Christ: Legalism, Antinomianism, and
   Gospel Assurance—Why the Marrow Controversy Still Matters* (Wheaton,
   IL: Crossway, 2016), 46.

ation. Of course, this is impossible in that we cannot account for *every* situation; however, the situations that an adherent has accounted for are no-brainers. Simply follow the previously thought-out rule for said situation. Life is so much simpler if one can blissfully flip to the right page of the rule book to answer challenging situations. Much of life is built this way. For example, sports adhere to previously laid out rules otherwise they quickly devolve. Break the rules and there are consequences. That said, if we spend enough time learning the rules and what they look like on the court/field, we can follow the rules without even thinking about it. Of course, one challenge to this is the volume of rules for a complete legalistic moral system is *massive*. The Pharisees, for example, added some fifteen hundred laws to prevent people from breaking the Law. Memorizing and actually doing that many laws gets very difficult. Nevertheless, the concept of legalism as a moral system itself remains simple.

It Is Easy to Know Where One Stands

If each and every situation has a rule associated with it, then it is easy to know how well one is doing morally speaking. We can simply look at the list of laws laid out and compare how well we follow them. Interestingly, this happened in Scripture. The parable of the rich young ruler in Luke 18:18–30 tells of this. A rich young ruler comes and asks Jesus what he must do to inherit eternal life. Jesus tells him that he needs to obey the commandments, to which the young man replies that he has done so, even from his youth. He had compared his life to the Law and found himself worthy according to the rules laid out there. Of course, Jesus then tells him that he still lacks one thing. He tells the young ruler that he must sell his possessions and give to the poor and then follow Jesus. The specific problem here will be looked at in greater detail later on; however, the fact of the matter is that the rich young ruler was easily able to know where he stood in regard to the Law. The Apostle Paul makes the same claim. He says of his pre-conversion self, "As to righteousness under the law, blameless" (Philippians 3:6). He was blameless when compared to the law.

Emphasizes Obedience

This last one is both a positive and a negative. The negative aspect of this will not be addressed just yet. When it comes to God's law, obedience is the answer, period. Legalism rightly makes this emphasis. God very clearly *expects* obedience. James 1:22, for example, says, "But be doers of the word, and not hearers only, deceiving yourselves." It is not the lot of humans to reject God's law. While God gives the free will to reject his law, doing so has dire consequences both in this life and the next. Legalism can be a force that fights against this.

CHAPTER THREE

PROBLEMS WITH LEGALISM

I N THE PREVIOUS SECTION, the positives of legalism were addressed, and it was found that there are indeed some valuable points.[1] However, legalism also has some very significant problems.

Focus on Rules Rather than One's Heart Condition

To begin with, legalism is an ethical system that does not care about our motives whatsoever. Someone could be considered extremely moral through this system by what they do even though they could be downright *evil* in their thoughts. Legalism simply does not care if a person *wants* to murder every man and rape every woman they have met so long as they do not actually perform the deeds themselves. This scenario is highly unlikely since someone like this person is almost certainly acting on their desires in some way

---

1. Though, these points also come with their caveats.

and would thus be immoral under legalism, but the point still stands. It is, fundamentally, focused on the *outward* signs of one's morality rather than one's inward motivations. Luke 18:10–14 is a parable of Jesus that demonstrates the folly of this. It starts, "Two men went up into the temple to pray, one a Pharisee and the other a tax collector" (Luke 18:10). The Pharisee begins praying and listing how much better he is than others, including the tax collector next to him, saying, "I fast twice a week; I give tithes of all that I get" (Luke 18:12). The tax collector, on the other hand, would not even lift up his eyes to heaven but instead cried out, "God, be merciful to me, a sinner!" (Luke 18:13). Jesus says that this tax collector is the one who went to his house justified rather than the Pharisee. The tax collector's heart condition was conducive to being justified while the Pharisee was justifying himself based on his adherence to rules sans humility.

It Is Completely Inflexible

Legalism as an ethical system suffers from being inflexible. It cannot adapt well to new situations. As mentioned in the last section, the Pharisees were an excellent example of legalism. Under their leadership, the Jews were burdened by extra heavy loads of rules that needed to be adhered to or else they risked breaking the law. Jesus attacks this directly in Mark 7. He says, "You have a fine way of rejecting the commandment of God in order to establish your tradition!" (Mark 7:9). Jesus goes on to give a specific example of how the Pharisees got around giving back to their parents by giving to God what would have been given to them and thereby circumventing God's command to honor one's parents. The religious leaders were essentially playing "Calvinball" from the Calvin and Hobbes comics. This is a game where the players can make up new rules as they go. Humans are not to add to God's law in such a way as to get around it. However, it is important to note that some of these additional rules and laws were placed on the people at least partly because Scripture "does not always address an issue clearly, if at all."[2] In order to have a legalistic system work, one necessarily must add rules on top of rules so that everyone knows *exactly* what they must do. This means that if there is a situation that is *not* precisely spelled out, legalism gives no valid way for an adherent to confront the problem. Normal people must wait for the elites to come up with new rules for this problem.[3] Additionally, there is no wiggle room for error. One follows the rules of legalism, or one is immoral. There is no in-between.

It Is Unbiblical

This will be a brief engagement here as the next chapter deals with a more robust discussion of what Scripture

---

2. Scott B. Rae, *Moral Choices: An Introduction to Ethics* (Grand Rapids, MI: Zondervan Academic, 2018), 110.

3. In the case of ancient Israel these elites would have been the Sanhedrin which is made up of the Pharisees and Sadducees.

teaches about sin and obedience to God.

Joel 2:12–13 says, "'Yet even now,' declares Yahweh, 'return to me with all your heart, with fasting, with weeping, and with mourning; and rend your hearts and not your garments.'" Legalism does not properly address what God is saying here. In fact, God is directly arguing against legalism in this passage. He does not want torn garments as a "sign" of turning away from sin. Rather, he wants his people to rend their hearts by changing how they live because they are truly remorseful. It is not merely the outward expression that matters. To be sure, this would *involve* actually doing things like fasting or even tearing one's garment; however, God is not seeking a behavior change devoid of a heart change.

Similarly, Jesus' teaching on anger and lust during the Sermon on the Mount (Matthew 5:21–30) directly argues against legalism. He makes a couple of seemingly radical statements on these topics. Instead of merely stating the rules that murder and adultery are evil and must be avoided, he states that even being angry with a brother or lusting after a woman in one's heart is enough to constitute sin. This is actually a demonstration of the first problem with legalism as a system from a biblical perspective. It is not the *physical* act of murder and adultery (or any other sin) where sin begins. To be sure, these things are sins, and legalism rightly says that one is to not do these things. However, legalism does not properly address the problem of a man's heart. This is exactly what Jesus is getting at in his sermon. A person's *heart* is the place where sin begins. Legalism cannot reasonably deal with this. It can only apply rules that *might* deal with the symptoms of a bad heart posture. For example, a king could force all women to wear baggy clothes and veil their faces to try and prevent men from having lust for women who are not their spouses. This is basically what the hijab (both the garment and the style of dressing) is for. Iran, for example, requires the wearing of a hijab for women. Theoretically, this makes it harder to lust after a woman as there is much less that can be seen. That said, it does not take much time on Google for someone to realize that the hijab *does not* solve the problem. Rape is fairly rampant in many Middle Eastern countries despite not being able to see much of the women in these countries. This is simply because the problem lies in the hearts and minds of sinful people. Actions come from within. This is why Jesus says, "The good person out of the good treasure of his heart produces good, and the evil person out of his evil treasure produces evil, for out of the abundance of the heart his mouth speaks" (Luke 6:45).

CHAPTER FOUR

LEGALISM, AS A SYSTEM, SHOULD BE REJECTED BUT THERE ARE VALUABLE ASPECTS

T HE ABOVE DISCUSSION DEMONSTRATES that legalism has some valuable aspects but ultimately fails to be a system that can be reasonably adhered to by Christians and non-Christians alike. What, then, should be done with it? Should it be rejected outright, or can one learn from it?

God Hates True Legalism

The starting point of this discussion has to be with God. What is God's view of legalism? Well, he *hates* it. Legalism is a perversion of what he desires. Yes, God desires "godly offspring" (Malachi 2:15). He desires those who follow his commands and legalism does make an effort to follow said commands.[1] That said, since legalism does not care about our heart posture as we go about this obedience, it fails to hold to what God expects. The prophets were regularly given a message of God's hatred and rejection of legalistic practices of continuing to offer sacrifices to God while the hearts, minds, and actions of the people were opposed to God.[2] In response to an attack on his character due to hanging out with "tax collectors and sinners," Jesus says, "Go and learn what this means: 'I desire mercy, and not sacrifice'" (Matthew 9:13). This is pulling from Hosea 6:6 which says, "For I desire steadfast love and not sacrifice, the knowledge of God rather than burnt offerings." Doing the right things *for the right reasons* is what matters to God.

God Loves Those Who Obey Him

While it is true that God hates true legalism, legalism does get one thing right. God is to be obeyed. Not only that, but God loves those who obey him. When God commands humans to do X, Y, and Z and not do A, B, and C, he expects obedience—in fact he *commands* obedience. Humans are not at liberty to disobey without consequences. The whole of the gospel is based on this very idea. God is

---

1. At least this is true to an extent. The Pharisees often used their own rules to get around God's commands. See Matthew 15:1–20 for an example of this.

2. Jeremiah 6:19–20, Isaiah 1:11–15, and Amos 5:20–21 are good examples of this.

holy and perfect and cannot stand sin. Humans sin and are unable to live a life worthy of gaining admittance into his presence. Thus, God sent his Son to die in the world's place as a perfect sacrifice to make a way for sinful humans to be brought into his presence. It is expected that non-Christians disobey God; however, Christians are commanded and expected to obey God in every area of their lives. This emphasis is something legalism gets right. The problem lies in the reason behind said obedience.

CHAPTER FIVE

LEGALISM PROVIDES A NEEDED COUNTERBALANCE TO SITUATION ETHICS

U P TO THIS POINT, we have only looked at legalism. That said, a common, modern-day counter to legalism is situation ethics. I would argue that these two systems balance each other out fairly well if one does a decent job of rejecting the bad and holding to the good of the systems.[1]

What Is Situation Ethics?

Situation ethics is a relatively new addition to the field of Christian ethics that was introduced by Joseph F. Fletch-

---

1. While I believe this is true, we should not be basing our ethical and spiritual decisions on these two systems. Our basis is God's Word. What I am arguing is that these two systems each hold some truth on making ethical and spiritual decisions. As such, if we reject the anti-biblical aspects of the systems, we can come to a decent method for making good decisions but, like I said, we should base our ethical decisions on Scripture rather than external ethical systems.

er in his book *Situation Ethics: A New Morality* which
was originally published in 1966. It was *quite* controversial
when originally published and still evokes debate from both
adherents and opponents.[2] It holds sway in many Christian circles today because it is based on love. In situation
ethics, one is expected to make an ethical determination
of what would be best in a given situation based on the
situation itself and what "love" would do. As such, every
situation should have a different ethical response and thus
there is no overarching system of rules to guide someone.[3]
Unfortunately, this system actively allows or even encour-
ages one to disagree with God's Word in many situations
if the situation seems to call for it. For example, Fletcher
states, "The new morality, situation ethics, declares that
anything and everything is right or wrong, according to
the situation."[4] This is fundamentally against God and his
Word. In situation ethics, love is supreme, but as Robertson
McQuilkin and Paul Copan point out, love is an arbitrary
attribute of God to focus on.[5] The problem with focusing

---

2. Joseph Fletcher, *Situation Ethics: The New Morality* (Louisville, KY:
Westminster John Knox Press, 1997), 1.

3. Steve Wilkens, *Beyond Bumper Sticker Ethics: An Introduction to Theories
of Right and Wrong* (Downers Grove, IL: InterVarsity Academic, 2011),
174.

4. Fletcher, *Situation Ethics*, 124.

5. Robertson McQuilkin and Paul Copan, *An Introduction to Biblical Ethics:
Walking in the Way of Wisdom* (Downers Grove, IL: InterVarsity Academic, 2014), 173.

on love is that it is subjective if taken on its own. We can justify all kinds of immoral things on the basis of love. For example, if a man knew that a single woman was desperate to have a child, he could justify sex outside of marriage with her, or even rape her, simply because of "love."[6] Norman Geisler gives lying as another example. He writes, "Love is the only absolute, and lying might be the loving thing to do. In fact, lying to save a life is the loving thing to do. Hence, lying is sometimes right."[7] *If* one were to properly define love according to Scripture and truly maintain that understanding in any given situation, then situation ethics would have merit.[8] As it stands, however, it is a completely subjective ethical system. This is especially true today since "in a culture infatuated with autonomy, personal experience and individual preference become the arbiter of what is true and right."[9] The autonomy of the individual is highly valued and sought in most Western nations.

---

6. This example is, of course, not demonstrating real love. That said, if an arbitrary view of "love" is all that is required in situation ethics, then one can reasonably label pretty much *anything* as love and get away with it.

7. Norman L. Geisler, *Christian Ethics: Contemporary Issues and Options* (Grand Rapids, MI: Baker Academic, 2010), 20.

8. Interestingly enough, this understanding would necessitate knowing the commands of God, including the Law, and properly applying those commands. So, while one could potentially make an ethic on the basis of biblical love, it would still not be truly "situational" as love is spelled out in Scripture under specific commands.

9. Stanley Hauerwas and Samuel Wells, eds, *The Blackwell Companion to Christian Ethics* (Malden, MA: Blackwell Publishing, 2006), 158.

How Does Legalism
Counterbalance Situation Ethics?

Though Fletcher argued that situation ethics is a middle ground between legalism and antinomianism, it is also the opposite of legalism in many ways.[10] Legalism creates rigid rules that must be adhered to while simultaneously failing to effectively address new or unique situations. In contrast, situation ethics has no structure (except "love") and necessarily expects adherents to modify their ethics based on each and every situation. Overall, each of these approaches to morality has some truth. Where situation ethics fails, legalism can, in a way, pick up the slack and vice versa. For example, situation ethics denies that there are correct answers to any given situation. This is valuable to understand in that *some* situations do not have a direct, biblical answer. However, legalism rightly counters this by acknowledging that there *are* correct ethical answers. Murdering someone is *always* a problem. There is no valid ethical way to murder someone. There can be ethical ways of *killing* someone (i.e., in self-defense or when commanded to by God), but this is different from murder. Thus, both situation ethics and legalism can be used to try to balance the other out. That said, merely attempting this balance is going to fail to

---

10. Fletcher, *Situation Ethics*, 26. Antinomianism *is* the true polar opposite to legalism; however, situation ethics is also effectively legalism's opposite. It only has one law and it is love.

produce a good and effective ethical system.

From Ethical Systems to False Gospels

The above discussion has primarily focused on legalism and situation ethics as ethical systems (i.e., ways of determining right and wrong behavior). However, these systems don't remain confined to ethics. When internalized deeply, they begin to shape how people understand salvation itself. In fact, the ethical framework one adopts often becomes the foundation for their view of righteousness before God.

Legalism, at its core, is more than a moral code. It is a theological claim. It says, "I can be justified by what I do." If legalism is rigid in ethics, it is even more so in its view of salvation. Obedience is no longer the fruit of faith or love for God; it becomes the very means of earning his favor. Righteousness becomes transactional: follow the rules, and God owes you something. This mindset is deadly because it replaces relational covenant with impersonal law. The legalist does not necessarily need to love God; he simply needs to perform. But Scripture flatly rejects this idea: "For by works of the law no human being will be justified in his sight" (Romans 3:20). Paul goes so far as to call this system a curse (Galatians 3:10).

Situation ethics falls into a different trap. While legalism exalts the rules, situation ethics exalts personal sincerity. It assures the sinner that as long as they "meant well" or "acted in love," God will be pleased. But love, divorced from the commands of God, becomes subjective and malleable. And when applied to salvation, it fosters a sense of self-justification based on emotional intent rather than obedient faith. This is no less dangerous. Jesus says, "If you love me, you will keep my commandments" (John 14:15). Rather than separating love from obedience, he binds them together.

Both systems, then, present a distorted path to salvation. Legalism offers salvation through external conformity. Situation ethics offers salvation through internal sincerity. But both replace the biblical gospel with a man-centered substitute. One says you are saved by effort, the other says you are saved by feeling. Neither proclaims the truth that salvation comes through faith in Christ and this faith must necessarily produce obedience even though said obedience never *earns* salvation.

Many Christians fear that emphasizing obedience will collapse into legalism, while others fear that rejecting works altogether will slide into antinomianism. This confusion is not academic; it cuts to the very core of the gospel.

The goal of this book has been to dismantle legalism as an ethical and salvific system. The next step is to ask what comes in its place. Can we articulate a biblical view of salvation that affirms grace, demands obedience, and avoids both extremes? The next chapter briefly engages with this, but these are the questions taken up much more robustly in *Salvation by Faith Alone?* There, we will look carefully at what Scripture actually teaches regarding faith, works, justification, and what it truly means to follow Christ.

This discussion is not about getting the balance right

between two flawed systems. It's about recovering the truth of God's Word and the gospel it proclaims. Legalism and situation ethics both fail because they are both, ultimately, centered on man. The gospel, in contrast, is centered on Christ. And that changes everything.

CHAPTER SIX

A BETTER WAY

I F MERELY BALANCING LEGALISM and situation ethics fails to produce a good and effective ethical and salvific system, what can? It is important to look to Scripture on this. Colossians 3:23–25 gives a good answer. It says,

> Whatever you do, work heartily, as for the Lord and not for men, knowing that from the Lord you will receive the inheritance as your reward. You are serving the Lord Christ. For the wrongdoer will be paid back for the wrong he has done, and there is no partiality.

This passage gives both the command and expectation to do good and the *why* and *how* of going about it. Rae puts it this way, "The emphasis is on obedience to a Person, not just to a command."[1] Of course, in some regard at least,

---

1. Rae, *Moral Choices*, 75.

this is limited to Christians. However, the moral concept behind it works out somewhat for non-Christians. People should desire to do, and actually do, good things simply *because* it is morally right. It is evident that, aside from those who have neurological disorders, humans know right from wrong. For example, the idea of a "moral compass" is widespread. Though this analogy can be used for relativism, it is better understood as a compass that always points toward moral truth. One might not *follow* the compass, but they *know* the direction of truth. For example, though there are and have been attempts to justify murder in various contexts, most people would agree that it is wrong.[2]

Ultimately, the passage above only makes true sense from a believer's perspective. Our love for God is what ought to drive us to live morally. The passage tells Christians that they are to do *everything* as though it were an act of service to God. On this passage, N. T. Wright states, "The task may appear unimportant or trivial, but the person doing it is never that, and he or she has the opportunity to turn the job into an act of worship."[3] This concept is all throughout Scripture and may be most directly laid out in John 14:15 which says, "If you love me, you will keep my commandments." In their book *Reclaiming Pietism: Retrieving an Evangelical Tradition*, Roger E. Olson and Christian T. Collins Winn write, "Evangelicals believe these

---

2. Robin Gill, *Christian Ethics: The Basics* (New York: Routledge, 2020), 22.

3. N. T. Wright, *Colossians and Philemon: An Introduction and Commentary* (Downers Grove, IL: InterVarsity Press, 1986), 153-54.

two dimensions—doctrine and devotion—belong together for holistic, authentic Christian life."[4] This is what John 14:15 is talking about. Right belief and devotion to God are wrapped together in love. Put differently, it is impossible to love God without obeying his commands. But this verse also implies that *love* is the reason behind the obedience. It is right belief (knowing the commands and expectations of God) followed by obedience *because* of one's love for God. This needs to be attempted carefully, however, as it can lead to legalism if one is not careful. In fact, it has been argued, likely correctly, that the legalism of the Pharisees started with proper motivations.[5] They likely added all the additional rules out of sincere love for and devotion to God. The lesson to be learned, then, is to adhere to the rules of God out of sincere love and devotion to him while not *adding* to his command, especially when said adding is done in an attempt to circumvent God's decrees, which is what ended up happening with the Pharisees.

What, Then, Is the Main Problem with Legalism?

As we can see from the previous section, legalism shouldn't

---

4. Roger E. Olson and Christian T. Collins Winn, *Reclaiming Pietism: Retrieving an Evangelical Tradition* (Grand Rapids, MI: William B. Eerdmans, 2015), 182.

5. Jerram Barrs, *Delighting in the Law of the Lord: God's Alternative to Legalism and Moralism* (Wheaton, IL: Crossway, 2013), 128.

be rejected outright. To do so leads to antinomianism. Instead, we can recognize that there are valuable aspects of legalism that we can hold to in order to avoid throwing out the baby with the bath water. That said, what made Jesus so mad about legalism? Why did Paul strive in his teaching against the idea that we can *earn* our salvation via works? The problem is that legalism is fundamentally a false god. True legalism (as opposed to allegiance to Jesus as king which necessarily involves obedience) holds rules up as god. It is the rules themselves that make someone worthy of heaven regardless of one's belief in God and obedience to him. This wrong focus, along with the fact that no one can actually satisfy a legalistic moral system, is why good works alone cannot save us. Salvation has *always* involved faith in the one true God. There is no other way. Legalism, then, is a false religion that leads to death. Understanding this makes it very easy to see why God and the apostles were so strident in their objections to this system. Likewise, Christians ought to vehemently reject legalism. However, too often Christians *do* throw out the baby with the bath water in their rejection of legalism by then completely rejecting works as being part of salvation despite the nearly overwhelming biblical evidence to support the notion. We must not make this mistake.

CHAPTER SEVEN

CONCLUSION

L EGALISM DOES INDEED HAVE some positive aspects. It rightly emphasizes obedience to God and gives one a clear understanding of where one is on the side of morality. Yet, these aspects are countered by much more significant problems, the most obvious of which is God's hatred for true legalism. Overall, it is clear that legalism ought to be rejected as a valid ethical system. Instead, one ought to live a life devoted to God via right understanding and practical application of said understanding. Obey God out of love for him and do good to others out of obedience to God and love for them.

But this raises an unavoidable and often neglected question: *If obedience is right, if it is necessary, and if legalism is wrong, then how exactly does obedience relate to salvation?* In other words, if legalism is a false system that tries to earn God's favor by rigid rules, but obedience is still required by God and commended in Scripture, then what role—if any—do works actually play in our salvation?

For many Christians, this tension remains unresolved.

In rejecting legalism, they have mistakenly embraced lawlessness. In avoiding works-based righteousness, they have embraced a works-free salvation. But Scripture does not give us that option. Jesus does not say, "If you believe in me, you'll go to heaven regardless of what you do." He says, "If you love me, you will keep my commandments." Paul does not argue that obedience is irrelevant. He frames his entire theology around the "obedience of faith." James does not pit faith and works against each other. He shows they are inseparable.

Legalism is not the problem because it commands obedience. It is the problem because it replaces God with rules. But a life of obedience rooted in love for God—submitted to his Word, dependent on his grace, empowered by his Spirit—that kind of obedience is not legalism. It is worship and a demonstration of faithfulness.

The question now becomes: Can a person be saved without that kind of obedience? Can faith truly save if it bears no fruit? These are not questions that can be brushed aside with theological slogans or pious assumptions. They are central to the gospel itself.

In *Salvation by Faith Alone?*, we will take up these very questions head-on. We will examine whether Scripture truly teaches that salvation is by faith alone, and if not, what it actually teaches about the nature of saving faith, obedience, and the role of works. We will not return to legalism, but neither will we embrace the shallow gospel of passive belief. If Scripture presents a better way (and it does) we must have the courage to follow it, wherever it leads.

A BRIEF CALL TO ACTION

If you found value in this book, please consider leaving an honest review on your favorite book review site (Amazon, BookBub, Goodreads, etc.). Reviews are tremendously helpful to authors. They are, in many ways, the lifeblood of a book and I highly appreciate each one that I receive.

Also, if you are interested in receiving updates on books, book reviews, and other short teachings that I publish, you can follow me on:

- Facebook (Meta): L. J. Anderson at www.facebook.com/profile.php?id=61553506423559

- YouTube: L. J. Anderson at www.youtube.com/@ljandersonbooks

- My website: www.ljandersonbooks.com

ALSO BY L. J. ANDERSON

Books

- *Contending for the Truth: A Biblical Look at Thirteen Contentious Doctrines*

- *The One Truth: Contextual Absolutism and the Battle for Doctrinal Clarity* (coming soon!)

- *Salvation by Faith Alone? Living in the Nuance of Faith and Works* (coming soon!)

The Triptych Theology Series

- *The Silent Killer: Religious Freedom and the War on the Church*

Short Academic Books

- *Theology and Apologetics: An Examination of How and Where They Intersect*

- *The Moral Argument: Is It Worth Having in Your Apologetic Repertoire?*

- *The Inerrancy of Scripture: An Overview and Defense*

- *Tribulation as Wrath: Rethinking the Timing of God's Judgment*

- *Hebrews 6:1–8: An Exegetical Strike Against Eternal Security* (coming soon!)

- *Gnosticism: A Biblical and Historical Response* (coming soon!)

BIBLIOGRAPHY

Barrs, Jerram. *Delighting in the Law of the Lord: God's Alternative to Legalism and Moralism.* Wheaton, IL: Crossway, 2013.

Ferguson, Sinclair B. *The Whole Christ: Legalism, Antinomianism, and Gospel Assurance—Why the Marrow Controversy Still Matters.* Wheaton, IL: Crossway, 2016.

Fletcher, Joseph. *Situation Ethics: The New Morality.* Louisville, KY: Westminster John Knox Press, 1997.

Geisler, Norman L. *Christian Ethics: Contemporary Issues and Options.* Grand Rapids, MI: Baker Academic, 2010.

Gill, Robin. *Christian Ethics: The Basics.* New York: Routledge, 2020.

Hauerwas, Stanley, and Samuel Wells, eds. *The Blackwell Companion to Christian Ethics.* Malden, MA: Blackwell Publishing, 2006.

McQuilkin, Robertson, and Paul Copan. *An Introduction to Biblical Ethics: Walking in the Way of Wisdom*. Downers Grove, IL: InterVarsity Academic, 2014.

Olson, Roger E., and Christian T. Collins Winn. *Reclaiming Pietism: Retrieving an Evangelical Tradition*. Grand Rapids, MI: William B. Eerdmans, 2015.

Rae, Scott B. *Moral Choices: An Introduction to Ethics*. Grand Rapids, MI: Zondervan Academic, 2018.

Wilkens, Steve. *Beyond Bumper Sticker Ethics: An Introduction to Theories of Right and Wrong*. Downers Grove, IL: InterVarsity Academic, 2011.

Wright, N. T. *Colossians and Philemon: An Introduction and Commentary*. Downers Grove, IL: InterVarsity Press, 1986.

ABOUT THE AUTHOR

L. J. Anderson is an independent scholar, author, and founder of **Lamad Press**, an academic imprint dedicated to publishing biblically grounded theological works. He holds a Master of Divinity and is currently pursuing a PhD in theology, where his dissertation research focuses on developing a new model of God. This model seeks to offer a coherent and biblically faithful framework capable of addressing longstanding challenges to the doctrine of God—particularly those related to the Trinity.

This work represents a piece of that broader research agenda, contributing to the reevaluation of traditional theological formulations in light of Scripture. Anderson aims to bridge the gap between philosophical coherence and scriptural fidelity, crafting theological models that remain both rigorous and accessible.

He has published several books through Lamad Press, including *Tribulation as Wrath* and *The Silent Killer*, and his writings are indexed in Google Scholar. As a disabled veteran, he is able to devote his time to research, writing, and publishing, with the long-term goal of establishing Lamad Press as a trusted source for independent academic theology.

He is also the founder of **Lamad Christian Books**, a curated online bookstore offering academic and devotional Christian works, Christian fiction, and clean non-Christian fiction. You can learn more at **ljandersonbooks.com** and **lamadpress.com**.

NOTES

FOR INSIGHTS, CONVICTIONS, OR FOLLOW-UP STUDY

www.ingramcontent.com/pod-product-compliance
Lightning Source LLC
Chambersburg PA
CBHW051336120626
46547CB00016B/2571